The Road Map to Senior Care

By Stephen Andriko

SUCCESS ALWAYS!

Stephen Andriko

Published by Stephen Andriko
Seabrook, Texas

First Edition

ISBN 978-1-105-91169-9

To my mother Emogene Andriko, 85 years young!

ACKNOWLEDGEMENTS

The inspiration to write this book grew from a four part article I wrote in early 2012 titled "Silver Alert-Is that My Loved One?" That article first appeared in WomansInSite.com, for which I would like to thank Kathryn Wheat and Cindy Dennen for giving me my start. With much encouragement from colleagues, family, and friends who saw a need to share this information with others, it grew into *The Road Map to Senior Care.*

I want to thank my co-workers, industry professionals - and mostly the families I've met through this journey that have allowed me to share in their loved one's care and who were the inspiration for this book.

Special thanks go to Professor Frank E. Wagner, Psy.D. for his editing and critiquing assistance.

My love and gratitude go to my wife, Judith, for her support and help during the entire process of bringing the book to print.

CONTENTS

CHAPTER 1

The Task Ahead

Those who find themselves in the "sandwich generation" are struggling with commitment to both younger and older family members who need their attention. Often the more significant challenge presents itself when senior family members have needs.

While the catalyst to act on behalf of our younger loved ones appears rather obvious, the same understanding of when to intervene in senior affairs can be perplexing. How does one step up to parents to tell them that they need care? What are the care options? Are there any resources to help in this process? Finally, and perhaps the cause of the greatest angst, how are we going to pay for whatever care may be appropriate?

Perhaps you are acting on behalf of a spouse in need of care considerations. These same issues present themselves. You may be even more emotionally challenged due to the extended length of time you have been committed to the well-being and happiness of your loved one.

Long-term care is generally a continuum. It starts at one level then advances as needs increase. Many people are thrust into that gamut without guidance regarding where to start and how to proceed. Specific traumatic events may trigger the search for solutions and thereby cloud the judgment of the seeker. The goal of this book is to alleviate the role of emotion in the decision-making process when considering the need for care and the subsequent evaluation progression.

I intend to lay out your options and also warn you of some common pitfalls. It is up to you to decide what to do in your specific circumstance. There is no right or wrong solution. The worst response, however, is to not do anything. Thus if you think something needs to be done – do it.

CHAPTER 2

Indications for Action

When to take action to acquire care for the benefit of a senior loved one such as a parent, grandparent, or maybe even a spouse can be quite difficult to discern. The most obvious situation has been observed by most of you on the freeway. If you are driving by one of the electronic billboards citing "M*issing Elderly...*" and that person could be your loved one, it is definitely time to step up and get some assistance. Situations short of that may be more complex in the determination process.

If your loved one presents a danger to themself or others then it is time to act on their behalf. Some issues may involve physical mobility and result in frequent falls or other physical mishaps. Perhaps Mom or Dad cannot get around the house with difficulty, or they have trouble cleaning up, preparing meals, or dressing themself without help. Many times those circumstances are rather easily identified and addressed.

However, issues involving the mental state of your senior loved ones can be much more challenging to identify. How do you decide if certain behavior is merely old-age forgetfulness or dementia that can provide a ripe environment for a broad range of dangerous possibilities?

Warning Signs

First let's examine what is dementia. Dementia is a group of symptoms resulting from the death of brain cells due to a variety of conditions such as Alzheimer's disease and other types of memory impairment. Most often the person exhibits loss of memory, reasoning and planning ability, along with changes in behavior.

Of course we are all a little forgetful from time to time. This condition is more consistent. The first cognitive functionality to disappear is the ability to plan for the future and execute those plans. As an example you set a date with your mother to pick her up at her place at 11AM on Friday to go to lunch. You arrive and she is not dressed and knows nothing about your lunch plans even if you try to remind her of the conversation you had when you made arrangements. Once is no big deal, but beware if this becomes a prevalent occurrence.

Another indication of dementia involves discussion of loved ones that have passed away as though they were still alive. The progression of dementia almost always claims memories in reverse chronological order from their formation. Thus your loved one knows that certain people exist in memory, but the dying event has been erased. In your loved one's mind they are still with us.

Behavior changes can also provide early warning. Is your loved one suddenly mean and short with you when that type of behavior has never been commonplace? You may have to trust your instinct regarding behavior issues. If you think it is abnormal, it likely is abnormal. These warning signs are certainly not all-inclusive. Indeed they may not even present danger at that immediate moment. However, you do not want to stop by to visit mom and find her captured by the television while in the kitchen a pan is burning on the stove. Of course mom is unaware. Or perhaps dad has driven off in the car and it has been a few hours since he had contact with anyone. You wouldn't want him to be the subject of one of those roadside billboards mentioned earlier!

Personal Observation

A common thread involving the warning signs involves personal observation. Many times children do not live in proximity to their senior loved ones. You may have to rely on a sibling or other relative who lives close by to provide timely and specific reports on the current status of your loved one. You might even involve neighbors and friends to obtain relevant information.

Do not fear asking for help in that observation process. It is better to gather information to assist in formulating care decisions than to have those decisions thrust upon you by a traumatic event. Parents are highly unlikely to voluntarily share their dementia related events with their children.

If You Suspect Action is Necessary–It Is!

While this list of potential symptoms and behaviors is not exhaustive it will give you a starting point from which to proceed. If you think that your loved one's issues demand further consideration, then act on those thoughts and devise a plan. You should always try to avoid having a traumatic event force a plan of care. Take your concerns to the next level; visit a clinical professional. It is much better to be safe than sorry. I am confident that for every senior identified in the electronic billboard, "Missing Elderly…" there is a family who recently had a discussion as to - "What should we do about Mom, Dad, Grandma, etc." Now that family is kicking themselves that they did not heed the warning signs to take action.

Appropriate Physicians

Now that you have decided to take action where do you turn? Take your concerns to the next level and first seek professional clinical advice. It is important to find a good geriatrician if your loved one is not currently under that level of physician care.

While some may consider their own family physician to be qualified to follow this clinical matter, they should consider a similar thought process that they employed when they selected care for their children. These days many parents choose pediatricians for specialized clinical expertise. Remember why you chose a pediatrician for your children? In turn, the special training and experience of a doctor who treats seniors is invaluable. Your family physician, insurance plan, or the internet may be available sources to find the right clinician.

Your loved one's memory issue might be as simple as adverse medication interaction - or as extensive as Alzheimer's disease, but you need a professional opinion. Your geriatrician may also recommend a neurologist if dementia is present. The neurologist can evaluate a variety of brain disorders and order tests that can point to a more specific diagnosis such as Alzheimer's disease. Once the geriatrician, and/or other consulting physician, has completed the appropriate evaluations, he will be able to provide ammunition to convince your loved one of the care necessary. After all, you can then explain, "The doctor says…"

CHAPTER 3

In-Home Care Options

So you have crossed the threshold of needing care. The next step is determining whether care should be provided in the home or outside of it. Even more variations loom beyond that basic decision. If you choose the in-home route, then you can opt for personal care (you do it) or professional care (hire someone).

Personal Care

If you provide personal care, be careful to consider the physical and emotional commitment necessary. It may merely require you to drop by mom and dad's house periodically to clean up or run errands. On the other hand your senior loved one may require as much care as your child does. In that case, it is a full-time commitment involving days, nights, and weekends regardless of your own needs or issues. Because of the demands of time and personal supervision, it is very likely that you and your senior loved one will need to reside together - maybe at their home or yours.

If you haven't already, you probably will soon realize that providing personal care for your loved one is an exhausting endeavor. It may also be even more challenging based on the "family" verses "public" persona of your loved one. Family dynamics generally follow a pattern in which the seniors are treated with love and respect, but they hold the authority power. When the time arrives for the younger to care for the older there may be some subconscious reluctance to reverse the roles. While you are trying to be as helpful as possible, there are some intimate issues that might be involved such as bathing and toileting assistance. Even if the situation involves one spouse caring for another, these highly personal events can create angst. Indeed, your loved one may be more compliant when dealing with a complete stranger than a family member providing the care.

While on the subject of spouses caring for other spouses, I would like to caution you that statistics indicate that the person providing the care is likely to pass away before the spouse receiving the care. Individual health issues that may exist prior to the beginning of the process do not affect these statistics.

If you decide that personal care is not for you, then you can select a professional care-giver. Please check your "guilt feelings" at the door. Remember your decisions should be based on what is best for the one needing care. If you abide by that concept throughout the care continuum then you are destined to be successful.

Professional In-Home Care

At this point you also have options. You can contract for care through a licensed agency that employs bonded professionals that have been extensively screened and specially trained. Their hiring and supervisory procedures are detailed in scope. Such agencies employ rigorous hiring policies that include criminal background checks among other criteria. They provide comprehensive training for personnel before sending them into a care-giving environment. They also have more than one care-giver covering a geographic area so that you need not worry about personal time off, illness, or a specific individual. An agency will work diligently to provide the same care-giver all of the time so that a rapport may develop with your loved one. You will be given the opportunity to meet with agency supervisory personnel and the specific care-giver to discuss your loved one's unique situation. Include questions about the agency's experience with your specific issue during the evaluation meeting. Many agencies specialize in care for those with dementia. Feel free to ask for a reference list if they do not provide one initially.

Some of you may opt to find your own care-giver. Keep in mind all of the criteria that you would include when selecting a sitter for your children plus a whole host of other considerations specific to your senior loved one's need. You can, and should, check the criminal background of a prospective applicant even if you know that person. Please ask about prior experience. You should not fear investigating the applicant's physical stamina that may be necessary to accomplish all of the care provisions.

Once you have chosen the most appropriate agency or person, you then must consider how much care is necessary. Again it could be as minimal as once or twice a week to help with basic chores of household living or as significant as 24-hour care services. You may want to blend your personal care with the professional care. Perhaps you have dad living with you, but you need a break periodically for personal events. If you choose to provide care on your own, be aware that it is a physically, emotionally, and spiritually challenging task and you may not get the recognition that you deserve and may expect for your efforts.

Home Health Care

There is another option to consider for in-home care when specific medical attention is necessary. That service is called Home Health. Home Health providers can arrange for a skilled clinician (think "nurse") to visit the residence of your loved one for specialized care. Several examples of this kind of care can be imagined such as a post-surgical wound care or physical therapy. Often these therapies will be prescribed by a doctor after care events such as a hospital stay and perhaps temporary residence at a rehabilitation facility. Those options will be discussed in a later chapter. Many more medical services can be provided in the home. Remember, the geriatrician is an expert in the field. Therefore, ask him or her about all of your options.

Agencies providing this type of care may also provide the non-medical care previously mentioned. You may be able to consolidate your options. The medical care provided by home health professionals not only is set apart from non-medical home care by the actual degree of assistance provided, but also by the source of payment for such services. The payment structure and options will be discussed in greater detail in Chapter 6. For now, understand that most clinical services, whether provided in the home or in a facility, may fall under Medicare for reimbursement. Non-medical care demands a different payment method.

CHAPTER 4

Out-of-Home Placement

The second option is care outside of the home. Here once again you have two basic categories, full-time or part-time

Adult Day Care

Part-time care is generally provided in an Adult Day Care environment. This setting may be at a church, community senior center, or licensed professional setting. Check with your local community resources to find available options.

Generally, community resources, such as a city or municipal Senior Center, are only provided for active seniors without special care needs. Churches and other charitable organizations may offer more robust care for those requiring some level of personal care. Keep in mind that the primary role of most adult day care is to provide social interaction and cognitive stimulation for seniors.

You can also contract with a professional community for such services. A fee-for-service adult day care establishment will exercise the same process in screening and training care-givers as professional home-care agencies. They will likely hold a license or certification depending on individual state requirements. These organizations certainly may provide an invigorating environment to meet the needs of your senior. They will provide a social environment as well as mentally stimulating activities to meet those challenges of your loved one.

Beyond that, since you are paying a fee for service you can expect to use this as a "sitter service" and respite while you attend to personal or profession demands such as running errands or your own job. Once again one may blend the adult day care program with personal in-home care to achieve the required level of care. Some adult day care centers even specialize in care for those suffering from dementia issues. Their programming provides activities and events specifically tailored to compensate for a loss of cognitive skills.

Many people ultimately choose full-time, out-of-home care. Arriving at this decision may be an evolutionary process involving all of the situations cited previously. However, there are even more options to explore.

Hospitals

First, hospitals provide a form of out-of-home care. Generally, the stay in the hospital is rather finite, depending, of course, on the reason for hospitalization. This type of admission is commonly called an acute-care stay and is initiated by a physician. The purpose for mentioning hospitals in a long-term care book is that there are several such facilities offering special consideration for seniors. They may have a senior-specific care division within the building itself with specially trained staff and providers. They may even have a senior care program designed to assist patients experiencing mental, emotional or behavioral needs. This service setting is often called a "Geri-Psych Unit" which is a common healthcare term for Geriatric Psychological Care. I have visited hospitals that even have a special Senior Emergency Room. This type of specialized service seems to be a trend in healthcare delivery. You should check with your geriatrician to see if such services are available in your area.

The needs of the patient's condition upon release from a hospital will determine the next step taken in the care process. One can categorize the hospital stay as a launching pad for long-term care.

Those needs will be evaluated as a result of care-plan discussions among a group of individuals concerned about the patient's care. First, the physician or perhaps multiple physicians will have an input. The hospital will assign a case manager who is familiar with the broad spectrum of discharge options as their representative. Of course the patient and patient's family have a say-so. However, if dementia is involved, the patient's input will need to be discussed with other family members.

Those options discussed may include the following:

- Long-Term Acute Care Facility-LTAC

- Skilled Nursing Facility-SNF

- Assisted Living

- Back home with care provisions

Long-Term Acute Care Facilities

While hospitals address acute conditions, they are generally designed to aggressively treat a patient. When that person sufficiently recovers, they relocate the individual to an appropriate environment for a more lengthy care regimen. When the patient's condition demands acute care for an extended period a Long-Term Acute Care (LTAC) facility may be recommended. Medical management, by a physician, of complex conditions is the primary deciding factor for evaluation of LTAC services. Generally, rehabilitation services are not the primary focus for LTAC patients. Physical and emotional comfort is therefore a key element of this type of care. Payment for care in an LTAC is generally prov

Medicare in similar fashion to a hospit.

Skilled Nursing Facilitie

Residence at a skilled nursing facility ı ᴜst similar to what your senior loved one may refer to as "being placed in a home." However, today's skilled nursing facilities bear little resemblance to that description. There are three basic reasons that a patient may be admitted to a skilled nursing facility. The first reason is that the level of clinical care required demands that type of environment for implementation. The second reason is that the patient requires rehabilitation therapy after an acute-care hospital stay. Finally, if the patient requires long-term care and personal funds are not available to pay for that care, Medicaid may provide funding in a skilled nursing environment. Further discussion of State-administered Medicaid programs can be found in Chapter 6.

Skilled nursing facilities are designed to provide nurse-supervised clinical care on a 24-hour basis. They treat relatively simple medical conditions that require less intensive therapy and do not demand direct medical management by a doctor.

Skilled nursing facilities often provide short-term rehabilitation following an acute care hospital stay for such things as surgery or stroke recovery. The time periods involved for rehab stays vary depending on the course of therapy. Medicare guidelines will determine the exact length of stay. Some skilled nursing facilities provide both in-patient and out-patient rehabilitation programs. A key advantage of this service is that highly effective care can be continued by capitalizing on the patient/therapist relationship built during the initial stay. Of course this is only valuable if the patient has the ability, proximity, desire, and transportation means to continue the out-patient relationship.

Funding for this type of long-term care may force that senior to reside in a Skilled Nursing Facility if Medicaid is the only source of payment. State guidelines will play a significant role in the Medicaid qualified facilities.

Medicare may participate in payment for the rehabilitation care. Medicare payment coverage may demand a patient copayment as length of stay progresses beyond the first twenty days of care. For more information regarding what Medicare covers contact a Medicare representative by phone or via the Medicare web site. The Medicare web site is listed in the Professional References section. More financial considerations are discussed in Chapter 6.

Often the extent of in-patient therapy depends on approval by Medicare for the funding of continued therapy measures. Several factors are considered in such decisions including patient progress and the continued need for services. Thus a family may find themselves in a situation where the rehabilitation facility suddenly informs the family that their loved one is being discharged in a day or two. Therefore, one should consider the next step in the care option continuum very soon after rehabilitation commences. Are you going to send your loved one home with care services (personal or professional), or are you going to opt for long-term out-of-home placement?

Assisted Living Communities

Assisted living communities provide care for seniors with needs for activities of daily living (ADL). Those activities include such things as grooming, dressing, bathing, meal preparation, cleaning, among others.

These communities vary in the levels of care that they provide. However, the residents generally live in a smaller apartment or bedroom. Some communities offer accommodations that may have a companion arrangement similar to a dorm room. Within the larger community, one finds common areas for dining, activities, and general socialization.

One variety of such a community is known as a Residential Care Home (RCH) or perhaps Personal Care Home (PCH). These home-style settings are quite personalized, and are even located in typical family neighborhoods. An RCH is often a house that has been transformed into a care environment with on-site staff to provide assistance with the ADL. Residents live in the bedrooms, either privately or shared, and utilize the common areas with other residents. Many families choose this type of environment because it presents a more intimate setting and may be less expensive than a larger community.

Some communities provide specialized memory care for those with dementia. The dementia care may be in a separate wing or building close to or attached to the main area. Opting to evaluate a community that provides both general assisted living and specialized memory care may be an advantage for seniors whose condition and symptoms have not advanced to the point that a secure environment is necessary. That individual can then "age in place" while moving from one environment to another within the same community. In such a case a physical move into a secure area may be necessary, but the family will already have a strong relationship with the management of the community. They will similarly trust in the quality of care based on personal experience with their loved one.

Additionally, if the care plan involves a couple and one does not experience dementia, then a community such as this offering both types of care may be more appropriate. That way, each person may physically reside in the more appropriate physical environment, but they can still share in many daily activities due to the close setting.

There are communities that are dedicated specifically to memory care residents. My own senior community where I gained most of my experience in senior care, the **Barton House** in Sugar Land, Texas, is one of the quality establishments providing excellent care for those with memory and cognitive impairment such as Alzheimer's disease. Evaluation of communities that specialize in memory care can prove advantageous since that is their area of expertise.

At senior communities like the Barton House, patients with dementia are THEIR business; their ONLY business!

Retirement Communities

If hospital visits can "launch" the need for long-term care, then retirement communities are often the precursor to such care. Many communities exist that refer to themselves as "retirement living." Some are merely homes or condos in a deed-restricted neighborhood catering to a senior population. Others are senior apartments again offering living arrangements for a more mature clientele. Most commonly, however, the identification as a retirement community cites a social living environment where seniors reside individually but interact in a common section of the community. One could think of this setting as a cruise ship that never leaves dry land.

You choose your own apartment, sized and priced for your specific needs. However, you eat in a common dining area and enjoy numerous social activities with other community residents. One begins to capitalize a variety of services that are somewhat care-oriented. As mentioned, meals are provided. Social activities abound both on the property and remotely during group excursions. The community cleans and maintains each individual apartment as well the common grounds. Many communities even provide personal transportation services, affording the opportunity to "give up" the car keys.

Some broad-reaching properties are classified as Continuum of Care Retirement Communities or CCRCs. They not only fulfill the retirement living concept, but they also provide the previously mentioned long-term care services on different sections of the property. They may offer the full, or partial, line of services including: Retirement Living, Assisted Living, Specialized Memory Care, and Skilled Nursing. The primary advantage of this type of community is the opportunity to "age in place" in the broadest sense.

Many people choose to reside in a retirement community because they can turn over household chores to others. Beyond that aspect, there exists a particularly mind-enriching benefit from living in the social environment. Social interaction is one of the best ways to exercise the brain. This brain activity can help ward off dementia effects for some time even in people predisposed to debilitating brain disease such as Alzheimer's. While brain exercise does not provide a cure, it may keep one functioning better for a longer time period in a similar fashion as cardiovascular exercise helps to limit heart disease. Those with loved ones living alone may want to consider retirement living as a health benefit for them.

Evaluating Care Communities

It is incumbent on you to visit the communities that you are evaluating to see if their care provisions meet your loved one's needs. Many families suspect that this type of long-term care will ultimately be necessary but do not actually visit communities until a physical or emotional trauma forces action. Keep in mind that the best time to evaluate communities is when you do not yet need them, so that you can remove emotional stress from the decision.

The first element to consider is the physical layout. Is the community appropriately cleaned and maintained? If the place has a significant odor when you visit then that odor is probably not a one-time event. Ask yourself such questions as, "Would I want to live here? How do the care givers interact with my loved one? Is this community too big or small for my loved one?" Since food will be a significant aspect of your loved one's continued care, you should evaluate that provision with a cautious eye. You may even want to schedule a meal for yourself or even your loved one, if appropriate.

Try to arrange your initial visit when personnel of competent authority are available at the community. The need to have the right person present to answer your questions or to address your concerns outweighs any desire for a surprise effect. You can always return unannounced when the field of communities is narrowed.

Remember to put the needs of your loved one in the forefront of your evaluation. This consideration is often set aside when families encounter distance issues in the process. Of course you and other family members will want to visit your loved one at their new residence. Your confidence in the ability of the selected community to deliver the highest quality of care that you demand should outweigh a few more minutes of drive-time to visit.

Perhaps hours of travel may be excessive, but a car trip is still an event, unless you are literally going across the street.

Trust your instinct when evaluating communities. You will generally find a place that just feels right.

Hospice Care

The final leg of the long-term care journey involves end-of-life care. Professional assistance is available for families dealing with this issue. It is called Hospice Care. Hospice organizations also subscribe to the process of employing specifically vetted and highly trained individuals experienced in handling the unique factors encountered in this most difficult of times. Hospice Care is, however, somewhat different because the care can be delivered in a variety of settings. One may move their loved one to a special in-patient Hospice facility. Additionally, care can be provided right in the home or even at a long-term care community such as skilled nursing or assisted living. Once again your geriatrician is a great resource involving this type of care.

Memorial Needs

Since we are already exploring emotionally charged issues, let's briefly address the finality of the care process. What do you do after your loved one passes? Hospice providers can assist in the mechanics of this activity, but you need to address the emotional aspects with appropriate family members to be totally prepared. Many seniors who are not challenged by care considerations plan for this with spouse interaction well before death is eminent so that the survivor is not making decisions in an emotional state. The same approach should be followed even when a loved one is cognitively challenged. The best time to evaluate such options is when they are not yet needed. Try to avoid the scenario where grief-struck family members are asking each other, "Did Dad want to be buried or cremated?"

CHAPTER 5

Resources to Help

The task of evaluating professional options for care may seem quite daunting. *It is*, but you can find help.

Revisiting the discussion of the experience and expertise of the geriatrician offers you one avenue for help. Beyond the doctor, there exist several other resources to provide very detailed or merely general support.

Geriatric Care Management

Geriatric Care Managers are professionals skilled in exactly this sort of evaluation process. They have intimate knowledge of a wide variety of care providers in a specific geographic region. You can search for one near you. Check the Professional

References section of the book for the general website listing. Those care managers provide their services for a fee paid by you, the person searching for care. The assistance that they provide can be quite comprehensive. It may even include accompanying you on visits to agencies or communities. Their specific fee schedule may dictate the scope of participation

Internet Based Resources

There is also on-line "matchmaking" organizations that can help find a community or care agency for your loved one in a specific geographic area. Many have a national presence so they can assist even if you are looking outside of your immediate surroundings. Often times that aspect is important to families particularly when different siblings reside apart, or when the senior in need is remote from the primary investigator. They know the communities from personal visits and can get you pointed in the right direction based on care needs and family budget.

These organizations do not charge you for their services. However, they do not work for free. Their fees are paid by subscribing senior care agencies or communities when care services begin. Some of you may have experienced this type of payment structure when searching for a new job. Often it is called using a "head-hunter." You can think of these groups as senior care "head hunters." While such an arrangement may provide for your exact needs, remember that not all of the communities or agencies subscribe to such arrangements, and may thus limit your options. Don't worry too much about unscrupulous activity though because these relationships are often monitored by state regulatory departments. The specific advisors that you encounter will often provide emotional support while assisting in the evaluation process from afar.

Elder Law Attorneys

Another vital resource is an elder law attorney. A broad spectrum of legal and estate issues loom when evaluating long-term decisions. A good attorney with strong experience in dealing with estate planning is invaluable. I highly recommend that you seek elder law services well in advance of care needs.

Of course most everyone is aware of the need to have a will in place. Beyond that relatively basic requirement there is a host of issues to address. Establishing medical and durable powers of attorney along with advanced medical directives are but a few of those tasks necessary to be completed while the person addressed in such documents still has cognitive authority to dictate such terms. These documents lay out the specific guidelines regarding who has the authority to make decisions for those who cannot decide for themselves due to physical or mental conditions.

Many legal considerations that may vary by State are involved. Thus, it is best to consult the Professional who regularly deals in such matters.

When assets are at stake, this need becomes more urgent. Your counsel can establish guidelines and financial vehicles to protect savings and still provide the funding for all of the costs of care that will be addressed in the next chapter. He or she may refer you to specialized trust officers from trusted financial organizations to assist.

Those middle-aged readers may find that a visit to an elder law attorney for your own interests may be in order in the near future. He or she may refer you to specialized trust officers from trusted financial organizations to assist.

CHAPTER 6

How Do We Pay for Care?

The big questions still looms. How does one pay for the care? Long-term care is far from inexpensive, but the alternative of perhaps seeing your loved one cited on the electronic billboard can be a strong counter-argument to care costs. Here are some of the price ranges for the various professional care options. These prices will vary by geographic location.

Care Cost Ranges	
In-Home Professionals:	$15-$25 hourly
Adult Day Care:	$50-$80 daily
Assisted Living:	$2,000-$8,000 monthly
Skilled Nursing:	$6,000-$10,000 monthly
Retirement Living:	$1,200-$6,500 monthly

Average Cost Ranges

In-home non-medical professional care costs range from $15-$25 per hour. Some negotiation can be effected for 24-hour care. You may find your own personal sitter at a lesser rate.

Adult Day Care runs $50-$80 daily. Many local community organizations that may provide a Senior Center for a variety of activities often charge an ongoing fee to use the Center.

Assisted living costs vary by care needed and specialization of the community. Costs will vary appropriately from $2,000-$8,000 monthly. Some communities may add additional charges for advanced levels of care. Ask before you get caught unaware. Opting for a companion room arrangement can lower the monthly fee if your loved one can tolerate such an arrangement. However, do not expect rates much lower than the $2,000 figure. Most communities charge a non-refundable, one-time community fee upon admission. That fee usually is in the range of $1,000 to $3,000.

Skilled nursing prices are from $6,000-$10,000 monthly (they usually cite daily charges so that it does not seem so ominous).

Retirement living has the broadest variance among the long-term options. Costs vary dependent on a variety of elements including: apartment size, property location, on-site amenities, the number of meals provided, and general social offerings. The prices range from $1,200-$6,500 monthly. These communities may require a "buy in" cost in addition to the monthly rent. That fee may vary from the tens of thousands to hundreds of thousands dollars. The buy in is designed to stabilize cost variance as one progresses through the care needs continuum. Many retirement communities treat that initial sum in different fashion. It may purchase a unit in the community or may merely be placed in an escrow account. The most important aspect to explore regarding any buy in is the return of money upon relocation or death. It is fitting to probe the subject vigorously as many readers have enjoyed or been dismayed when dealing with a similar situation involving vacation time-share property.

As with most prices you can attempt to negotiate costs for some out-of-home placement. Occasionally you can capitalize on a single-digit percentage reduction in price. Try the process with your selected community; the worst that could happen is that you pay list price.

Medicare Coverage

Medicare may pay for some short-term rehabilitation costs in a skilled nursing facility, but covers **no cost** for long-term care (room and board) in any setting. The payment structure for in-patient rehabilitation costs may require a patient copayment for care service periods beyond twenty days. Medicare may also pay for Home Health services, but not the non-medical home care costs. For the most part, these costs are paid directly by the family. However, Medicare does provide funding for Hospice Care. As you would expect, Medicare does provide coverage for most services at a hospital. For more detailed information concerning Medicare coverage visit the Medicare web site in the Professional References section.

Financial Resources for Veterans

Many families are unaware of the VA Aid and Attendance benefit for Veterans and surviving spouses. The benefit applies to Veterans and surviving spouses who require the regular attendance of another person to assist in bathing, dressing, meal preparation, medication monitoring or other various activities of daily living. This benefit is available to individuals who reside in assisted living communities, residential care homes, skilled nursing facilities and those receiving personal in-home care. There are three elements to qualify for benefits:

Basic Qualifications:

- Any Veteran with 90 days of consecutive active duty service who served at least one day during active war time. The Veteran did not have to serve overseas or in combat. Periods of War follow:

  - **World War II:** 12-07-1941 to 12-31-1946
  - **Korean Conflict:** 06-27-1950 to 01-31-1955

- - **Vietnam Era*:** 08-05-1964 to 05-07-1975 *Starts 02-28-1961 for those who served in the Republic of Vietnam
- The surviving spouse of a Veteran if married to the Veteran at the time of the Veteran's death and has not remarried.

- The spouse (who requires care) of a living Veteran even if the Veteran does not have care needs.

Medical Qualifications: One must provide proof showing that the applicant requires daily assistance of another person in performing routine activities of daily living due to an illness, injury, or mental capacity. This proof must be furnished by competent clinical authority such as a geriatrician.

Financial Qualifications: Certain income qualifications do apply. The applicant's income from all sources is compared to out-of-pocket medical costs to determine financial need. Those medical costs do include such things as unreimbursed medical expenses including insurance premiums, the cost of assisted living or nursing home care, or the cost of in-home care. There is no specific limit on how much net worth a veteran and his dependents can have, but net worth cannot be "excessive". The decision as to whether a claimant's net worth is excessive depends on the facts of <u>each individual</u> case. In most cases the VA does not consider the claimant's home or car an asset. Even if you believe you have too many assets to qualify, it would be advantageous to investigate this benefit option to be certain.

Payment Available if Qualified: These figures are the maximum amounts of eligibility in 2012. They are monthly figures and are tax-exempt amounts. Money is paid directly to the applicant's account or a designated financial party, such as a family member. It is not paid to a care provider.

- A Veteran - $1,704

- Surviving spouse of a Veteran - $1,094

- Married couple - $2,020

- Veteran is healthy but his or her spouse needs assistance - $1,338

How does one apply for benefits?

- Go to **www.va.gov** and use the Veterans On-Line Application (VONAPP).

- Contact your VA Regional Office.

- Utilize one of the many free veterans' service organizations that your selected care provider (in-home or out-of-home) may know in your local area.

You must be paying for care **before** you may apply! To say that the VA process is quite slow is a huge understatement. The good news is that once you are approved for benefits the payment is retroactive to the first full month following the date of application. Your first check may be thousands of dollars. While you await the VA payment you are responsible for the costs of care. Some financial organizations, such as banks, offer bridge loans to help while you wait. Terms of these arrangements vary. Check with your selected care provider to see if they can recommend anyone that they have used successfully in the past. See the VA web site listed in the Professional References chapter for further information about Aid and Attendance. Also your elder law attorney can provide assistance with the VA issues.

Long Term Care Insurance

Some of your senior loved ones may hold long term care (LTC) insurance policies. These policies are designed for exactly this kind of need. However, many older LTC policies were written when there really were only "nursing homes" available. When you investigate your loved one's paperwork you may want to consult a professional such as attorney or your own insurance agent to verify coverage concerns. At a minimum, call the issuing company to get clarification.

By the way, those of you gasping at the care costs cited might want to consider purchasing an LTC policy for yourself. Some policies written today may blend death benefits with long-term care coverage, offering you financial relief in case of death or life. If your senior loved one does not yet exhibit symptoms that demand care, he or she may still find a policy. Some LTC policies are written up to age 75.

Age and health of the covered person are very important in the price of a policy. The earlier you start the process the greater the advantage to your bank account. This investigation for your loved one or yourself demands consultation with a licensed agent.

Sell the Home

Many families decide to sell their senior loved one's property to help pay for care. Often the house has full equity value since the mortgage has been paid. Indeed, it has probably enjoyed a dramatic rise in value since purchased. Thus, the asset base created from the sale may last a long time. This is a good option for those that have only one surviving spouse living at that former homestead.

If both members of the senior couple are still living you can still exercise the property sale option, but you must realize that one person may not require care. They could potentially move in with you or another loved one. Additionally, there are some assisted living communities that can accommodate a couple. As with most anything else there is an increased price with two people involved.

A further option to investigate if you are looking to keep your loved one in the family homestead with professional care provision is a reverse mortgage. This transaction can be tricky to the unknowledgeable. Seek professional financial advice prior to exercising this option.

Medicaid

A final payment option rests with Medicaid funding. This is heavily based on financial need. Frequently, all assets must be liquidated prior to application for the approval process. Income limitations vary by state, but they do exist. Generally, there is a significant waiting list for care provisions from authorized Medicaid providers. You should check with your local county or state officials.

CHAPTER 7

Continue the Process

Care considerations can appear overwhelming. Remember to approach your fears for the safety and well-being of your senior loved ones in deliberate fashion. It is always important to consider what is best for the loved one in need. Emotional and financial considerations may impact your progress, but progress itself is very important. The most significant lapse in the entire process occurs when family members know that a problem exists, but avoid taking any action to help the situation.

Family meetings may prove necessary. That event may prove to be quite emotionally charged. Opinions may vary and tempers may flare. Suffice to say that the well-being of the one in need should be paramount in any deliberations. If you continue to bring discussions back to that premise, then you should enjoy success.

Just remember that electronic billboard, "M*issing Elderly...*' and keep that from becoming your loved one. As previously discussed, that family with a missing loved one is now painfully racked with guilt and remorse for not acting when the time was right. Do not allow that to happen to you.

RESOURCES

Elder Law
The American Association of Trusts, Estates and Elder Law Attorneys (AATEELA)
www.aateela.org

Geriatric Care
American Geriatrics Society
www.americangeriatrics.org

American Geriatrics Society for Health in Aging (FHA)
www.healthinaging.org

National Association of Professional Geriatric Care Managers
www.caremanager.org

Health Coverage
The Center for Medicare and Medicaid
www.cms.gov

Veterans Administration
www.va.gov

Long Term Care Insurance
National Society of Insurance Commissioners (NAIC)
www.naic.org

Senior Health
National Institutes of Health- NIH Senior Health
www.nihseniorhealth.gov

Alzheimer's Foundation of America
www.alzfdn.org

Alzheimer's Association
www.alz.org

ABOUT THE AUTHOR

Stephen Andriko grew up in northeastern Ohio. Upon graduation from high school, he earned an appointment and subsequently graduated from the US Naval Academy where he majored in mathematics. After graduation his military career continued with the United States Marine Corps. Eleven years into his career he was diagnosed with Type 1 diabetes which resulted in a medical separation from the Corps. After the military he became a highly successful sales and management executive in the Healthcare Industry. He is currently the Marketing Director for a memory care community in Sugar Land, Texas where he found his passion for senior care.